The POOR ROGUES HANG

POEMS BY THOMAS TYRRELL

MOSAÏQUEPRESS

First published in 2020

MOSAÏQUE PRESS
Registered office:
70 Priory Road
Kenilworth, Warwickshire
CV8 1LQ

ISBN 978-1-906852-53-5

Contents

Historical Note

Pirate stories have always been more than half legend, but this collection of ballads and verse tales has at least the merit of drawing directly upon the original versions, laid down in *The General History of the Robberies and Murders of the Most Notorious Pirates* (London, 1724). Credited to a Captain Charles Johnson, who some have suspected to be Daniel Defoe writing under a pseudonym, *The General History of the Pirates* inspired almost every poem here printed. The exceptions are 'Spoils and Division', which draws on Defoe's novella *The King of the Pirates*; 'Gráinne Ni Mháile', who was too good to leave out; and 'Old Boyce', who sailed into my dreams one stormy October and refused to weight anchor until the collection was done.

– TT, Birmingham, January 2020

The Preface

(*Johnson* / Tyrrell)

Having taken more than ordinary Pains
as flogging, revisions, keelhauling, writer's circles, running the open mic gauntlet and counting syllables on our remaining fingers

in collecting the Materials
as sea-rovers, scallywags, buccaneers, corsairs, marauders, plunderers, pillagers, picaroons, freebooters, filibusters and downright pirates

which compose the following History,
or collection of historical poems: as ballads, ballades, sapphics, sonnets, syllabics, vers libre, &c,

we could not be satisfied with ourselves,
no, by God!

if any Thing were wanting to it,
except, begging your pardons, mermaids, sea serpents, sirens, Captains Hook, Silver, Sparrow, Pugwash, or perhaps a Kraken,

which might render it entirely satisfactory to the Publick
those most notorious seafarers, land-lubbers, poets, rebels, prosers, villains, fighters, tyrants, heroes, cowards, lovers and downright pirates.

How They Set Out

The sailors packed the *Victoire's* deck from rail to polished rail
As Captain Tew addressed his crew. "We've orders to make sail
For factories on the Gambian coast and put them to the sword,
Pitting ourselves against the French for small or no reward.
They'd have us fight, not for our right, nor for our country's sake,
But for nabobs who'd never put their precious lives at stake.
If you'll be guided by my voice, we'll steer another course,
And turn our guns against all flags, a roving pirate force."
Unbroken save by creaking boards and by the lapping swell,
All down the deck, from stem to stern, uneasy silence fell
Until Jack Drake, the youngest there, went to the captain's side,
"A golden chain or wooden leg, I'll stand with you!" he cried.

Sensing that now the tide had turned, success was in his reach
The captain of the ship resumed his interrupted speech.
"Although the letter of the law would call these doings treason,
I've searched each tome of Greece and Rome and found no valid
    reason
Why wealthy knaves who trade in slaves (a practice I abhor)
Should hiss their fears in naval ears and send us off to war.
If they take all the benefit, and none to us remains
Then we are slaves ourselves, who dance to music of our chains,
And if beneath the Union Jack our lives cannot be free,
Then let us hoist a plain black flag and take up piracy."
A fair gust stirred the topsails, and before the breeze dispelled
"A golden chain or wooden leg!" a dozen voices yelled.

"If it should so content you that the captaincy be mine,
Each sailor here shall have a vote and articles to sign.
We'll all debate in council which way we should shape
    our course,
And I'll advise, but not command, the option I endorse.
Then, should we take a treasure ship, we'll never scrimp
    or hoard,
But dole it out in equal shares to every man aboard,
And we'll not stain our hands again with reeking
    senseless slaughter
But spare the lives of those we fight if they should cry
    for quarter.
If any man should turn me down, I'll put him safe ashore,
Who then will sail a-pirating beside me?" With a roar,
The officers and foremast hands took up the general call,
"A golden chain or wooden leg, we're with you one and all!"

Of Gráinne Ni Mháile

After Kate Garrett

To weave by hearth-fires she disdains,
Red locks cropped short against her skull,
The tameless oceans fill her brains,
Their cold salt spray, their fresh sweet rains,
Storms beat but cannot hole the hull.

Perched high while battle seethes below,
Red locks cropped short against her skull,
She sees the fight ebb to and fro,
Leaps down and deals the killing blow,
Storms beat but cannot hole the hull.

They raid the bays and prowl the shores,
Red locks cropped short against her skull,
Three galleys of a dozen oars
That fight for her and Connacht's cause,
Storms beat but cannot hole the hull.

Ringed round by brutal foes and mean,
Red locks cropped short against her skull,
She takes to sea, her true demesne,
Seeking the aid of England's queen,
Storms beat but cannot hole the hull.

Fine silks and rubies gleaming bright,
Red locks cropped short against her skull,
Beyond their meddling courtier's sight,
Two queens conspire by candlelight,
Storms beat but cannot hole the hull.

'My favour, grace and clemency,'
Red locks cropped short against your skull,
'I grant you, Gráinne Ni Mháile,
And I will see your son set free,'
Storms beat but cannot hole the hull.

Her family and lands secure,
Grey locks cropped short against her skull,
By no means gentle, chaste or pure
She has the worldly-wise allure
Of those who struggle and endure,
Storms beat but never holed her hull.

Of Captain Avery

Now gather round and lend an ear,
    for there's a ballad I would sing,
of famous Captain Avery
    and how he went a-pirating.

The good ship *Charles* lies in the port,
    her anchor's down, her sails are furled,
her Captain's snoring in his bunk
    dead drunk, and dead to all the world.

The crew creep barefoot cross the deck,
    weigh anchor softly as they might
and slip beyond the harbour bar,
    all in the darkness of the night.

The Captain feels the ocean swell,
    the surging as the sails are set.
He curses, spits, and rings the bell;
    half drunk and half asleep as yet.

"Now what's the matter with the ship?
    What weather is it? Does she drive?
A storm has blown us from our port
    or I'm the dullest dog alive."

"A damned dull dog you surely are,"
    the First Mate tells him to his face.
"You must walk out, and get below,
    for you are standing in my place.

"Damned impudence, you call it? Hush,
    a secret I will tell to you.
Your storm-lashed, flogged-out British tars
    are now my trusty pirate crew.

"We're bound for Madagascar shore.
    As gentlemen of fortune, we
shall make our fortunes, one and all,
    the gallant terrors of the sea."

He threw the captain in the launch
    with all who wouldn't join his band,
and cut them loose to winds and tides,
    far from the sight of any land.

And so the mutiny was done.
    Such is the ballad that I sing
of famous Captain Avery
    and how he went a-pirating.

Spoils and Division

They've taken a treasure ship of Spain
With twenty wounded, seven slain,
And aboard her they found, piled high in the hold,
A hundred and sixteen chests of gold,
With silver bar and fine wrought plate,
And each man grins and hugs his mate
As they leave the Spanish to weep and groan.
But the captain broods in his cabin alone,
For this is the way his thinking ran:

Six thousand pieces of eight a man!
It's a handsome hoard to behold.
With the clear sweet note as the coin rings true
And the gleam of the good Spanish gold.
But there's wild false light in the eyes of the crew
And it makes my blood run cold.
For now it's hornpipes, grog and song,
And it will be for many an hour,
But come daybreak, it won't be long
Before their mood grows sour.

Six thousand pieces of eight a man,
And all fellowship at an end!
For it's too much for men to risk their lives,
And it's too much to carry or spend,
But enough to make them wary, sly
And mistrust their closest friend.
How long till a card-sharp is seized by the hair
And stabbed for a gambling debt?
Or someone cries that part of his share
Was stolen while he slept?

Six thousand pieces of eight a man!
When jealousy starts to nip
Their flesh, they'll find it sufficient bulk
To make this handsome ship
A far worse hell than a prison-hulk.
For if any sailor should slip
Overboard, to splash his wealth ashore
How long till his tongue grows loose?
Till he sets the country on a roar
And we all go to the noose!

Six thousand pieces of eight a man!
Are we fortunate or cursed?
Now it's fitting their captain should be seen
But I'll prime my pistols first,
And keep my cutlass close and keen,
Lest things should come to the worst.
Oh, it's fine to sail a-pirating,
Dreaming of splendour and wealth,
But a bloody, savage, hellish thing
When a crew turns on itself.

A Syllabic Ballad of Captain Low

This is the ballad of Captain
    Ned Low, a real low cur:
the only pirate not to have
    a redeeming feature.

With his crew of bloodthirsty and
    violent men, this pirate
terrorised the American
    coast until the day that

Low in the *Fancy* and Harris
    in the *Ranger* were found
and engaged by Captain Peter
    Solgard of the *Greyhound*

in June 1723.
    Resolving to attack
Low hoisted his feared flag: a red
    skeleton on a black

background, and bellowed the order
    to fire. When the cannon
smoke cleared the decks were blood-soaked and
    Ranger's mainyard was gone.

Seeing his ally disabled
    Low decided to make
a run for it, sacrificing
    their lives for his own sake.

They, seeing their commodore flee,
    called for quarter and struck,
none of which was necessary;
    a leader with more pluck

would easily have sunk the man-
        of-war, but Low's courage
had broken, a thing he concealed
        by swearing in his rage

bloody revenge on all of the
        ships they met afterwards.
Their first prey they whipped round the deck
        then blew his skull to shards.

By their third victim their fury
        had cooled. As a result
he was only forced to eat his
        ears with pepper and salt,

which counts as getting off lightly.
        If you are wondering why
you've not heard of Low, his career
        was characterised by

torture and cowardice; unlike
        Blackbeard, Rackham or Tew
the swashbuckling romanticised
        look didn't stick. As to

how Captain Ned Low ended his
        life, we don't have a breath
of news: he doesn't even die
        a satisfactory death.

Anne Bonny to Captain Johnson

Now we are to begin a History full of surprizing Turns and
Adventures; I mean, that of Mary Read and Anne Bonny; the odd
Incidents of their rambling Lives are such, that some may be tempted
to think the whole Story no better than a Novel or Romance…
—The General History of the Pirates

Ah, Captain Johnson, our lives
were no mere amatorious novel,
unlike your Roxanas, Clarindas
and such drabs of the bookseller's stall.

I was pirate and woman and all,
and I sailed with and lay with Jack Rackham,
who, if he had fought like a man,
need not have been hanged like a dog.

And still a warm glassful of grog
or a lungful of salt air recalls those
fiery kisses from Jack and from Mary
and the tang of hot blood on the deck.

We left many brave warships a wreck,
many argosies spoiled of their cargo.
We were pardoned by Governor Rogers
but returned to our old course the same.

Beyond law, beyond guilt, beyond shame,
slipped free of the cables of duty,
we sailed by the wind and the starlight
and lived by the codes that we chose.

When the privateers, our foes,
found us moored off the coast of Jamaica,
the men fled below, drunk and fearful.
Only Mary and I stayed to fight,

and our cutlasses gleamed and flashed bright,
and our pistols roared out like the thunder.
We fought, back to back, for our freedom,
with our teeth and our nails and our knives.

I'm the only one now that survives.
The *Revenge's* crew went to the gallows;
Mary's dead in the jail of a fever;
I'm left with the memories alone,

the proud sins that I'll never atone
for, adventures not found in the pages
of your idle romances and novels,
the resort of the leisured and bored,

where the heroines find their reward
in making a dazzling marriage
to a cultured and virtuous husband
as their dainty and dutiful wives.

Of Mary Read

Kiss me Anne: the blaze of your mouth rekindles
fire and hope. To hell with our craven crewmates,
just as pirate-hunters have found and caught us,
drunken and useless!

Hanging frights me not in the least, but losing
you appalls me, Anne. Yet I'd alter nothing
had I power to abolish the laws that sentence
us to the gallows.

For, I think, if not for the noose, the oceans
were as choked with timorous rogues as England.
Merchant ships would hide in their ports and pirates
starve for employment.

We would never meet: I would still be fighting
for King George in Flanders, my sex unthought of,
you in marriage chained to a sailor-husband,
oceans between us.

Death makes ours a trade only fit for heroes
brave enough to bid all the world defiance,
brings together souls of the rarest temper,
hardy, ferocious.

Anne, mad Anne, the girl that I stole from Rackham,
know this now: however my death shall claim me
our last stand is all that my heart could wish for,
fighting together

back to back on deck in the vivid sunlight.
Let the boarders come; we'll display no mercy.
If this is the price of a pirate's freedom,
gladly I'll pay it!

Of Captain Vane

I.

Emerging from his sandy bed,
    his egg-bound form uncurled
the hatchling turtle pokes his head
    into the bright new world.
With scarcely opened eyes, he sees
a sight majestic even blurred:
his first dawn breaking on the cays
    and Caribbean swell,
brightening the palm-groves and the strands
gilding anew the golden sands,
    waking new life, as well
as gannet, gull and frigate-bird,
that throng the pink-and-yellow skies,
shrilling their raucous hungry cries,
eager to gorge themselves replete
on luscious tender turtle meat.

As when, among the clash and shout
of men killing and being killed,
retreat gives way to panicked rout,
the victors chase the losing force
and slaughter them without remorse,
their days cut short, their lifeblood spilled:
so down the strand the hatchlings flee,
    an urgent clumsy dash
towards the safety of the sea
    where breakers roll and crash.
Vicious as sabre, pike or gun
the cruel beaks claim them one by one,
    the seabirds swoop and dive.

Between the egg that gave them birth
and shelter in the foaming surf
an awful gauntlet must be run.
    Just one in ten survive.

Our turtle joins this desperate race.
His flippers thrust him down the beach
towards the azure dwelling-place
    almost within his reach.
A shadow flits above his head;
it seems his brief sweet life has fled
    and he is seabird's fare,
for gripping fast and holding well
two pincers seize his infant shell
    and hoist him in the air.
Between man's finger and his thumb,
he struggles, vehement but dumb.

II.

Sprawling upon the soft fine sand,
a turtle hatchling in his hand,
scratching his beard, the pirate mulls
    in idle reverie
whether to throw it to the gulls
    or toss it in the sea.
    And this is Captain Vane;
As ruthless as the frigate-bird
    he prowled the Spanish Main.
His ship swooped down on merchant prizes
filching their cargoes undeterred
    by any nation's law.

Amassing vast amounts of plunder
through pistol's bark and cannon's thunder,
his fearful reputation rises
　　for deeds of blood and gore,
till our notorious Captain Vane
was shipwrecked by a hurricane
　　on this unpeopled isle.
His crew all gone to Davy Jones,
their lone survivor warms his bones
　　beneath the sun awhile.

Eyes shaded by his battered hat,
all through the morning, out to sea
he gazes sadly, longingly,
at his old sloop—or rather at
the shadow of its shattered bulk,
the broken-backed dismasted hulk
that, in the last hours of the squall,
was wrecked upon the reef, with all
　　its stores and tools and freight
unreachable. Vane cannot swim;
he never learnt; it seemed to him
　　too much like tempting fate.

His restless soul receives no balms
from verdant groves of coco-palms,
or northern mockingbirds in song,
or multi-coloured fish that throng
the waters of the still lagoon
beneath the full-blown harvest moon,
or any wonder of creation.
A serpent in this paradise

inured to every kind of vice
he craves the violent stimulation
of cruel acts and bloody deeds
and other, even darker needs.
Far worse than hunger or distress
is his tormenting idleness.
It stirs him to the very core,
quickening his heart and breath
to hold within his palm once more
 the power of life and death.
"Dry land is perilous for you,
 as ocean is for me.
Why must I linger here, to rue
losing my fortune, ship and crew
 while you go swimming free?"

And with those bitter final words
he draws his forearm back to fling
the turtle to the hungry birds,
already waiting on the wing,
when suddenly, into his view
blows something wholly strange and new.
His nostrils flare; his eyes go wide;
out of his palm the turtle falls
onto the sands, and swiftly crawls
to safety in the swelling tide.
Oh, can his eyes be seeing true
 or do his senses fail?
No, there on the horizon's lip
beating towards him, comes a ship
 under a press of sail.

III.

"Damned if it isn't Charlie Vane!"
    the shout rings down the deck.
"I'd heard that you'd been hanged or slain
    or perished in a wreck.
How fares it with you, Charlie? Come
and drink a glass or two of rum."
And Captain Vane, bewildered, dazed
by clashing voices, almost crazed
by solitude, does as he's bid,
obedient as a calf or kid.
Before his senses are aware
he's settled in the cabin chair,
a glass of dark sweet rum in hand.
He sips, and as the spirit burns
down his parched throat, his strength returns,
his air of power and command.

    He draws himself up straight
and with shrewd eyes and ready wit
surveys the captain opposite,

    his former second mate:
a stolid, mild son of the sea
who looks at him as thoughtfully
as Vane, not half an hour past
looked at the turtle in his grasp.

"Holford! It's you, my fine stout-hearted
old shipmate! You've grown fat and thrived!
Who would have guessed when last we parted
we'd meet again some nine months hence
as I set sail from Providence

just as the Governor's ships arrived?"
And here Vane's tone of discourse hardens:
"Did all that scuttlebutt of pardons
    and governors amount,
in the event, to anything?
or do you sail a-pirating
    upon the old account?"

Holford meets Vane's appraising eyes
unblinkingly as he replies:
"No, things aren't as they were of yore.
A scallywag I sail no more,
    no more a buccaneer
since, for my crew and conscience sake,
King George's pardon I did take,
and rove like old Sir Francis Drake,
    a licensed privateer.
Governor Rogers wants you dead;
after you fired your prize and fled
he set a bounty on your head,
    a handsome sum in gold.
Your ship is but a shattered thing
that's hardly worth the salvaging
and you yourself, I'm sad to say,
a scrawny tattered castaway.
What can you offer me instead
    more than I now behold?"

Vane sensing with a stab of fear
that weakness would be fatal here
conceals it with a careless laugh.
"Why, you come on too strong by half!

You know as well as I
such freaks of luck are how things go.
Though now my fortune's sunken low,
    soon it will soar as high.
From the Indies to the Spanish Main
the merchant crews will quake again
to hear the name of Captain Vane
    and see my black flag fly.
I'll pay to you, in grateful duty
a third of all my future booty
if you will see me safe ashore,
    and work my passage too;
Morgan himself could ask no more
    than what I offer you."

Now Holford's face grows harsh and cold.
"I know you, Charlie Vane, of old.
Don't think to use me as your tool,
I'm not such an infernal fool
    as you would have me be.
I know I scarcely could afford
to have your wicked tongue aboard
    formenting mutiny.
And well I know I'd hardly live
the fortnight through, were I to give
    to you a seaman's berth.
And don't give me 'your sacred oath
of stainless honour' for we both
    know what your word is worth.
On this atoll, you're held as fast
as any man in prison cast
    so here it is you'll stay

till I come back the other way
and bear you off to Cagway Bay,
    to see you hanged at last."

Vane starts up with a roar of rage,
fierce as a tiger—but his cage
    is fastened and secure.
Before Holford can come to harm
two burly seamen seize each arm
    and drag him out the door.
A dagger pricks against his throat;
he's bound and tossed into a boat,
    and dumped upon the shore.

Catching the freshening western gale
the ship weighs anchor and makes sail
while from the headland's utmost spit
Vane's curses echo after it.
Trapped in the paradise he loathes
whose golden sands and citrus groves
enchant the eye but can't conceal
him from Holford when he comes back.
He seems to hear the flex and crack
of gallows ropes—can almost feel
    the noose around his neck—
as with her topsails flying free
the ship scuds swiftly out to sea.
    It dwindles to a speck
and with the sunset's final glim
slips under the horizon's rim.
So Vane is left, alone in night,
to make whatever peace he might.

And all that night, in fevered dreams,
he writhes and spasms, swears, blasphemes,
curses his fate but nothing seems
    to be of any use.
Through all the wastes of land and sea,
Holford pursues relentlessly;
Try as he might to struggle free,
    Vane cannot shake him loose.
However hard he tries to fend
it off, the winds and tides all tend
to his inevitable end:
    Jamaica and the noose.

A Cilician Pirate, 57BC

You say you are a man of Rome,
Brought up among her schools?
That city on the seven hills,
Where Julius Caesar rules, they say,
Where mighty Caesar rules?

Your pardon, sir! We'll cut you loose
To make your own way home.
We've sworn we'll never lock away
A citizen of Rome, oh no,
Never a man of Rome.

A noble Roman once set sail
With a princely retinue
And we boarded him and took his ship
And slaughtered all his crew, we did,
We slaughtered all the crew.

So haughty were his looks and speech,
Imperious yet handsome,
We saw at once that he was worth
A rich and golden ransom, yes,
A twenty talent ransom.

He laughed at our demands and said,
"You know not whom you hold.
For I will buy my liberty
With fifty talents in gold," he said,
Talents of purest gold.

Once freed, he hired himself a fleet
And sought us far and wide.
My shipmates he took prisoner
And had them crucified, he did,
Throats slit and crucified.

We hold no Romans ransom now,
But swiftly set them free.
The sea, they claim, is their domain,
We drop them in the sea, we do,
Headfirst into the sea.

Your liberty is now restored,
Walk out along this plank.
Swim home to mighty Caesar's arms.
It's him you've got to thank, oh yes,
It's Caesar you should thank.

A Frightful Ballad
Of The Third Lord Boyce

October winds, October seas,
    around the ship they seethe and roar.
John Graham, the third Lord of Boyce
    hears a knock on his cabin door.

"With compliments of Captain Spence,
    You're wanted on the deck,
to see a sight was never seen
    from Cape Town to Quebec.

"Your father's ship has come alongside
    and John Graham, the second Lord
of Boyce cries out in a fearful voice
    for you to come aboard."

The blood fell from Young Boyce's cheek,
    his heart was sore afraid.
"My compliments to Captain Spence,
    sure some mistake is made?

"My father's dead ten years this night,
    my father died at sea.
All souls aboard his ship were drowned
    in the storms of 'ninety-three."

"And was that ship the *Son of Eve*
    out of the Port o' Spain?
And did it have a figurehead
    bearing the mark of Cain?

"And is your father a red-haired man
    who stands full six-foot high
with a blazing cheek and a broken nose
    and a hellfire gleam in his eye?"

And then Young Boyce went up on deck
 to a crew half-mad with terror
and looking on his father's face
 he knew there was no error.

Old Boyce bestrode the quarterdeck;
 his cannons were shotted and rammed.
"I'll have Young Boyce to join my crew!
 Though we be cursed and damned,

"A man's own son, when all's said and done,
 should stand beside his sire.
So have Young Boyce conveyed aboard
 or else I'll open fire!

"And the salt sea-waves will be your graves
 and your daughters and widows will grieve."
With a single leap, Young Boyce spanned the deep
 and stood on the *Son of Eve*.

Young Boyce went to his father's side
 and clasped his outstretched hand,
as fiery red and burning hot
 as any cattle brand.

He made his quivering knees be still,
 he made his heart beat slow
and in a steady, offhand voice,
 he asked to go below.

"Oh, my young Boyce, you'll have the choice
 of cabin, as you ought.
A long, long trip you'll spend on ship
 'ere we come to any port.

"This night we sail the seas of earth,
    and feel the fresh west wind.
The Other Place has oceans too,
    though of a different kind.

"With a hot and sulphur-stinking breeze
    and a bitter, burning spray
where I and you and all our crew
    will sail till Judgement Day."

And then Old Boyce took up his lamp
    and led his son below,
where the lantern's gleams showed only scenes
    of horror, shame and woe.

Backs flogged until the ribs gleamed white
    and angry blistered burns.
Dead hopeless eyes, that haunt Young Boyce
    whichever way he turns.

But his cabin was filled with gold and jewels,
    the spoils of piracy,
with a narrow bunk and a cannon-port
    that looked upon the sea.

Here Old Boyce left him to his rest
    with the ghastliest of grins
and Young Boyce, sinking on his bunk,
    bethought him of his sins.

"In Paris and in London, I
    have lived a life of pleasure,
not thinking how my carefree wealth
    was blood-soaked pirate treasure.

"Not thinking how my father's wealth
    was buccaneering booty.
I sought not to redress his crimes.
    Alas! I shirked my duty.

"For these bright stones how many bones
    lie bleached and bare and dry?
For wealth untold of Spanish gold
    how many men must die?
What comfort can these trinkets give
    if I lose my soul thereby?

"Shall I sail aboard the *Son of Eve*
    on seas of grief and dole
or cast myself from yon cannon-port
    and swim for life and soul?

"Must I share the fate and bear the curse
    of my father and his men?
Oh, I'd rather brave the salt sea-wave,
    if my strength should fail—what then?

"Better lose my breath to a sailor's death,
    with Davy Jones to dwell,
than forever ride by my father's side
    on the fiery seas of Hell."

And men still speak of the thin white smile
    of his corpse as it lay on the shore,
like one who's braved Hell's worst and saved
    his soul forevermore.

The Last Speech of the Condemned Pirate

They were poor Rogues, they said, and so hang'd, while others, no less guilty in another Way, escaped.

—The General History of the Pirates

You gentlemen who are my jury,
These final words let no man gag.
I fought and drank with Captain Roberts
And sailed beneath the pirate flag.
My bread was spoil, my meat was plunder.
I rue it, but it comes no shock
To find myself a felon sentenced
To swing at Execution Dock.

I laughed to scorn the laws of nations
And though I fought fair and lived free
I did things that I quake to think on,
Deeds that will live in infamy.
And now, a man condemned, I stand here,
A flaming beacon on a rock,
Warning the mariners to windward:
Steer clear of Execution Dock.

For it's the same the whole world over,
The poor rogues hang; the rich rogues thrive.
While three tides toss my chained cadaver
Think of the monsters left alive.
The slavers, gorged with human cargo,
The managers of South-Sea stock,
How comes it they will never join me
To swing at Execution Dock?

Jurors, I go to death as blithely
As good King Charles went to the block.
Let no-one jeer me on my journey
To swing at Execution Dock.

Of Captain Gow

"Why, Johnny love, so bleak and dour?
You should be blithe and full of glee,
You've father's blessing on the hour
When you will marry me.

"When you were but a master's mate,
Long for my hand you moped and sighed,
And never thought I'd bide so long
To be a captain's bride.

"Now your fine ship lies in the bay,
A wondrous handsome sight to see.
Tomorrow you will ride to Kirk
And there will marry me."

"It drove me wrong, it drove me wild,
My jealous love so sorely tried,
And I grew mad with rage to think
You were another's bride.

"My dreams were haunted by your face,
All those long nights I spent at sea;
I swore a heaven-shaking oath
You'd marry none but me.

"Our captain would not sail us home,
O Christ! I shot him and he died.
Tomorrow, should you come to Kirk,
You'll be a pirate's bride."

"From Madagascar to St Kitts,
Or to the shores of Barbary,
I swore we'd never part again
Once you had married me.

"I'll board the quaking merchantmen
And wield a cutlass by your side.
My dearest love, I have no scorn
To be a pirate's bride.

"Until we've sailed, we'll cloak your crimes
In deepest shrouds of secrecy.
Unguessed at, we will ride to Kirk
And there you'll marry me."

Of Captain Davies

Gather around me then, if you would hear
A ballad of the famous Captain Davies,
That cunning and resourceful buccaneer,
The shame and scourge of French and British navies.

All down the Ivory Coast he robbed and fought,
Allied with pirates Cocklyn and La Bouse,
Until a rum-incited quarrel brought
An ending to that profitable cruise.

Then, braving many fearsome storms and squalls,
(The weather in that season blowing vile)
He reached a colony of Portugal's
Just off the Guinea coast, called Prince's Isle.

Pretending to be sailing in pursuit
Of pirates—murderous bloodthirsty ones—
He made the point, returned the fort's salute
And dropped his anchor underneath its guns.

His crew rowed him ashore with splendid show,
Their conduct rousing no suspicious fear.
The governor was not ashamed to know
The charming captain of the privateer,

Who bowed like a fidalgo at a ball,
Though all the while, with sidelong looks, he saw
How many muskets hung upon the wall,
How many guards were posted at the door.

The governor made him welcome to the port,
Let him refresh his stores and clean his hull,
And never guessed his newfound friend had fought
Beneath the black flag with the grinning skull.

As Davies watched and waited day by day,
A framework for the heist began to form.
He told his crew deception was the way:
"The fort's too strong for us to take by storm;

"The governor's our prize. I think we'd best
Lure him aboard, and when he's on our ground
We'll suddenly clap pistols to his breast
And ransom him for forty thousand pound.

"I'll send to him a letter, with at least
Twenty gold pieces and a dozen slaves,
Inviting him to share our parting feast
Before we set off on the ocean waves,

"And then we'll hold him fast." The pirates cheered
The clever captain of their scheming band,
Not knowing the discovery they'd feared
For all these weary weeks was close at hand.

One of those dozen presents was, he swore,
No slave nor chattel but a freeborn man,
So he slipped overboard and swam ashore
And told the governor the pirate's plan.

We like our pirates to be Robin Hoods
Fleecing the greedy empires of their gold,
Who don't look on their fellow men as goods,
Unfeeling chattels to be bought and sold.

While some escaped that harsh and servile fate
By learning how to fight, hand, reef and steer,
Like Caesar, who was Captain Teach's mate,
An old sea-devil with a long career,

Most of the wretches in the slaver ships
Were sold on, since the jangling of doubloons
Muffled the clink of chains and crack of whips,
Drowned out the weeping in the barracoons.

When Davies and his men arrived in town,
Ready to take the governor aboard,
They found an ambush laid to shoot them down
As outlaws, and to put them to the sword.

Cursing and bleeding, panicking, they fled
Back down the hill, all order lost, pell-mell.
A volley—and a dozen men lay dead.
Another volley—and their captain fell.

Like a game cock, that with its final breath
Claws at the victor, Captain Davies drew
His pistols from their holsters: each dealt death
To his pursuers and helped save his crew,

Who fled as he lay dying in the street.
And that's how Captain Davies met his end,
Struck down and thwarted in the final feat
Of trickery his wily wits had penned.

"Now this notorious pirate has been slain,"
The governor said, "our trade will soon revive.
Slave-ships will throng the harbor once again,
Our wealth will grow, and Prince's Isle will thrive."

As for the black slave, I can't tell you where
He was, or what he did, or how he felt.
Perhaps he fled to breathe a freer air,
Or went out with two pistols in his belt.

Of Major Bonnet

Retirement isn't suiting him, he finds.
There's open war between him and his wife,
but the begonias won't march in lines
like proper soldiers. Nothing in this life
amuses him or captivates his fancies,
not island gossip nor affairs of state.
Each evening he escapes into Cervantes
where Don Quixote and his squire await.
Increasingly with each page he discovers
his sanity envies their mad romance
of windmill-giants and enchanted lovers.
The candle gutters. He sits on entranced.
Into his melancholy reverie
arrives the thought: *There's always piracy...*

Of Captain Teach

SCENE: A low tavern on the seacoast of the Virginia colony.
CHARACTERS: Israel Hands, master; Samuel Odell, able seaman.

Hands
So here we are, the last two rogues unhanged.
Let's raise a glass of rum to Edward Teach
And the red hell he rots in.
      Odell

               Captain Teach!

[They drink and grimace]

Hands
Vile treaclish stuff.
      Odell

             Last time I drank that toast
Was in his very best West Indian rum
Aboard his ship the night before he died.
      Hands
First time you drank it too, I dare be sworn,
Or you'd be swinging in the gibbet chains
Like all my other shipmates.
      Odell

                Aye, that's true.
I came aboard by chance, not by free will.
Teach was the terror of the Outer Banks,
Exacting tribute with the governor's wink
From any ship his roving fancy took.
Our captain fenced it on for him, and I
Was pressed aboard *Adventure* on that voyage,
Seeing that Teach's hands were twenty short

Of complement. He feasted us that night
To make all right, not knowing that the sloops
Ranger and *Jane* were moored around the point
Preparing to do battle in the morning.

Hands

What thought you of our captain?

Odell

Why, his beard
Was everything I'd heard of it: thick, black,
Swathing his face up almost to the eyes,
And coiling down to sprawl across his chest
Like sinking smoke from cities set afire,
Its ends tied up in tufts. The eyes above
Were blue and bright as sapphires, but without
A glint of warmth or kindness. While we talked
If he grew red with drink, or pale with rage
I couldn't tell you, for the beard hid all,
Like ivy vines that swarm neglected walls
Making stone, brick, casements and porticos
One undistinguished mass of foliage.
He held his peace for most part of the meal
Until one man plucked courage up and asked
Him if his wife knew where his gold was hid.
His laughter chilled our blood as with an oath
He swore he'd bedded fourteen bouncing wives
In fourteen various ports, and whored them out
Among his crewmates on their wedding nights
After his lust was spent—but none of them,
None but the devil and the captain's self,
Knew where his treasure lay. Their bargain was
The longest-lived should have the lot, he said.

Hands

Still dreaming to outlive the devil yet.
For rule by fear I never knew his like.
Some held Old Scratch to be as much a shipmate
As Caesar or James Blake, and after Teach
Added him to the muster, hardly dared
To listen to the roll call lest a voice
Out of the air or sea should answer 'Present!'
What, do you smirk and sneer?

Odell

                                        Not I, I swear.

Hands

Perhaps you think the thing a parlour trick,
A show to awe pigtailed illiterates,
Not worthy of an educated man?
You never saw how quick his mood could change
From mirth to violent rage and back to mirth
Without a twitch or twinkle in his eye
To mark the shifting of the wind. Last time
I drained a glass of rum to Blackbeard's health
Was with the pilot of Pamlico River
As we sailed into Bath. That evening
He was the merriest of company.
We drank, and drank, and never saw he'd drawn
His pistols underneath the tablecloth,
Till with one breath he blew the candles out
And blew my knee to bloody smithereens.
The cabin was a chaos, dark as pitch,
Until Tom Miller brought in light and found
Me on the planking, howling out my pain,
The unscratched pilot wailing in his fright,

And Blackbeard screaming, for he liked the noise.
'Why, damn you all for sneaking craven whelps,
If I don't kill a shipmate now and then
You'd all forget the man you're sailing under!'
That's what he said, and while this knee of mine
Aches in the night and hobbles me by day,
I shan't forget to curse him.
Odell
                                    Cursing was how he died,
Breathlessly cursing as the lifeblood gushed
Out of his wounded neck; as the King's men
Closed in on every side, and their Lieutenant,
Who had been reeling, cutlass smashed in two,
Almost struck down, regained his squandered breath
And pressed his new advantage. In a cloud
Of powder smoke, among the clash of blades,
He fell with five shots in him and the marks
Of twenty cutlass blows. Lieutenant Maynard
After the rest surrendered, gave commands
For his decapitation, tossed the corpse
Into Pamlico Sound and had his skull
Lashed to the bowsprit like a figurehead.
So all our homeward voyage, beneath their flag
Of Britain and King George victorious
His beard and hair streamed out before the wind,
Black as his colours.
Hands
                        Back in Hampton Roads
I hear that Governor Spotswood stuck his head
Upon a spiked pole at the harbour mouth
To warn prospective pirates of the fate

Awaiting those who set the world at scorn
And plunder like free princes. Carrion crows
Pick his flesh clean, and use his famous beard
As lining for their nests.

Odell

                   And Teach's soul?
You think it's truly in the other place?

Hands

Why, when my knee is paining me of nights
I wish him truly damned as man can be.
Yet other times I fancy he escaped
The devil's clutches by some scurvy trick,
Clawed off a lee shore by the Cape of Hell
To sail with Avery and Henry Morgan
Into the sea of legends—damn his eyes!

Of Captain Kidd

My name is Captain Kidd, and God's laws I did forbid,
And most wickedly I did as I sailed.

—Old Ballad

As I was rowing down by Wapping
Coasting with the evening tide,
I sang a song of Captain Kidd
And how that pirate lived and died

Most wickedly, until a wailing
Cut across my jaunty tune.
A spectral figure stood mid-river
Between me and the rising moon.

His fine apparel hung in tatters,
Ooze was dripping from his bones,
Vacant sockets tracked my passing
As the captain's ghost intones:

"Three hundred years they've sung that slander,
Every boatman passing by!
Was there ever honest sailor
Wrecked upon so base a lie?

"Commissioned as a pirate hunter
I was sent from Plymouth Hoe
To hunt all Freebooters, Sea Rovers
And Frenchmen, as my country's foe.

"Deep-laden Dutchmen wallowed past us,
Riches crammed into their hold,
Argosies and lumbering galleons
Jingling with Indian gold,

"All Britain's allies, and to us
Forbidden fruit. Among the crew,
As we found no prize nor pirate
Discontented mutterings grew.

"William More, the wildest of them,
I kept beneath my scrutiny,
Knocking his brains out with a bucket
Before he roused a mutiny.

"Finally, a likely vessel
Redeemed our run of evil chance.
A merchant ship, and from her mainmast
Flew the fleur-de-lys of France.

"We fired a warning shot; the captain
Came to and hauled his colours down,
Brandishing safe-passage letters
Issued by the British Crown,

"At which I cursed, but could not rein in
My crew, nor call off their attack.
They ransacked her from bilge to bowsprit
And would not hand their booty back

"Harangue them how I would. We parted
That ship and mine, but to my cost:
The captain told foul tales about me,
My honest reputation lost

"All men now called me rogue and pirate.
The moment I returned to port
I was arrested and imprisoned,
And when my case came up in court

"My crew all swore false oaths and had me
Sentenced, spite of my just cries,
To the gallows and the gibbet
By their perjured wicked lies.

"At Execution Dock they hanged me,
Like one whom God and Man condemns,
At Tilbury Point they chained my body
To rot and moulder in the Thames.

"Would I had died to pounding guns
Or in the roaring of the surf!
And rested fifteen fathoms deep
Or six feet underneath the earth!

"Or would the homebound sailors gazing
On my sad corpse, knew what they saw.
No pirate, but an honest captain
Fallen prey to the devouring Law!"

Before my eyes the spectre vanished.
Too thunderstruck for sound or speech,
I watched the river in the moonlight
Glide the length of Wapping Reach.

Since then, I row not after nightfall,
Nor ever sing, as once I did
The ballad of that famous pirate,
The notorious Captain Kidd.

Pieces of Eight

I.   New-minted silver
        gleams in Columbus's palm,
        the argent *abuelito*
        of the $lick greenback.

II.   32x Real = Doubloon.
        16x Real = Escudo.
        8x Real = Real de a Ocho.
        Hence the name. Tail side,
        a ribbon sways between
        the pillars of Hercules,
        hence, so they say, the symbol.

III.   The mules were dying too fast,
        so behind the frontage of Potosí Mint
        enslaved Africans, *acémilas humanas,*
        turn the mills. Their blood and sweat
        give a queasy sheen to every coin.
        They are the engine of the currency
        by which their lives are bought and sold.

IV.   Spain's wealth is minted in the Indies:
        mined from the mountain that eats men,
        the ore is smelted, stamped
        with the face of a far-off monarch,
        shipped overseas.

V.   Jangling galleons set sail for Spain and Manilla:
        China accepts nothing else.
        Pirates and privateers
        circle them like sharks.

VI.   Alexander Hamilton (you know this tune)
       weighs the worn-out Spanish royals
       to set the purity of the U.S. silver dollar:
       the buck starts here.

VII.   In Oz they punch O's in Spain's old silver,
       making two coins from one: the holey dollar and dump.
       Profane shit and sacred silver,
       current in all realms.

VIII. Captain Flint the parrot screams
       and jerks Jim Hawkins from his dreams.
       Pieces of Eight! Pieces of Eight!
       In playgrounds children chant the words,
       Pieces of Eight!

Acknowledgements

Some of these poems have previously appeared in *Amaryllis, Dear Reader, Picaroon, Spectral Realms* and *Time & Tide: Stories and Poems from Solstice Shorts Festival 2019*.

Some of them were regularly heard at St Cannas Ale House open mic, First Thursday at Chapter, Room at the Top in Penarth and the now-defunct RARA. Many thanks to all involved in the organisation of these valuable venues and everyone whose enthusiastic support made me realise a book of pirate poems was a workable venture.

Personal thanks to Rahul Gupta, *il miglior fabbro*; Saoirse O'Connor, aspiring mermaid; Kate Garrett, for a ready-made venue; John Eliot, for his warm recommendation; to the Tyrrell family at home and to the Tyrrells over the water.

– TT

About the Author

Thomas Tyrrell lives in Birmingham, UK, a disappointingly long distance away from the sea. He compensates by affecting a distinctly piratical beard, though unlike Captain Teach he has yet to set it on fire. He has twice won the Terry Hetherington poetry award and is a regular and enthusiastic performer of his own work. He has a PhD in English Literature from Cardiff University.